*To: Ms Brenda Poledor—
Be Blessed!
vR
Mary G.*

Women Stop the Chase
Workbook

Let God's Man Find You
(Proverbs 18:22)

By

Dr. Mary M. Gillam, Col (Ret), USAF

Women Stop the Chase
Workbook

Let God's Man Find You
(Proverbs 18:22)

By

Mary M. Gillam, Literary Enterprise, LLC

Scripture taken from the Good News Translation (GNT) – Second Edition, Copyright 1992 by American Bible Society. Used by Permission.

Scripture taken from the New American Standard Bible®, Copyright © 1960, 1962, 1963, 1968, 1971, 1972, 1973, 1975, 1977, 1995 by the Lockman Foundation. Used by permission.

Scripture quotations marked (NLT) are taken from the Holy Bible, New Living Translation, copyright © 1996, 2004, 2007 by Tyndale House Foundation. Used by permission of Tyndale House Publishers, Inc., Carol Stream, Illinois 60188. All rights reserved.

Scripture taken from the Holy Bible, Today's New International Version™ (TNIV), ® Copyright © 2001, 2005 by International Bible Society®. All rights reserved worldwide.

Verses marked KJV are taken from the King James Version of the Bible. Used by permission.

Cover and photo by Create Space

Copyright © 2013 by Mary M. Gillam

All rights reserved. No part of this publication may be reproduced or utilized in any form or by any means, electronic or mechanical, including photocopying and recording or by an information storage and retrieval system without the prior permission of the publisher.

For additional books by the Author and booking information:

- ❖ http://MaryMGillamLiteraryEnterpriseLLC.com
- ❖ Dr.MaryM.Gillam@gmail.com
- ❖ gillammm@verizon.net

Printed in the United States of America

ISBN-13: 978-1490942681

ISBN-10: 1490942688

Dedication

To Almighty God who gave me the vision and privilege to write the book, *Women Stop the Chase: Let God's Man Find You*, and the accompanying *Workbook* so that it can inspire and motivate women to follow God's plan for relationships.

Acknowledgments

First, I want to personally thank everyone who has purchased and read the book, *Women Stop the Chase: Let God's Man Find You*. I have been overwhelmed with your generosity and favorable response. Several of you asked if there was an accompanying *Workbook* to the original text? I am elated to respond with a resounding, "yes." By the grace of God, I am proud to share this *Workbook* with each of you.

Second, I want to acknowledge many people from across the world that have inspired and encouraged me to share this message. Many of you have expressed the sentiment that had you known this information before, you would have made some different decisions in your life. My heart is humbled by what God is already doing with this work.

I pray that you will be blessed and that God will use you to be a blessing to others. Likewise, if you have already experienced God's favor in this area of your life, I encourage you to share your experience with others.

Table of Contents

Dedication vi

Acknowledgments vii

Table of Contents... ix

Chapter 1: Introduction... 1

Chapter 2: The Relationship Journey 7

Chapter 3: Trusting God with the Decision.......... 11

Chapter 4: Pressing into the Things of God 17

Chapter 5: God's Precious Jewel............................. 21

Chapter 6: Stepping Ahead of God?....................... 27

Chapter 7: Are You Making Yourself Discoverable? 31

Appendix A 37

Appendix C... 39

Appendix D 40

Appendix E 41

Appendix F 42

About the Author.. 43

x

Chapter 1: Introduction

This *Workbook* is designed to accompany *Women Stop the Chase: Let God's Man Find You* which is based on Proverbs 18:22, *"He who finds a wife finds a good thing and obtains favor of the Lord"* (NASB). History records that this proverb or moral adage was penned by King Solomon who excelled in wisdom. *"And God gave Solomon wisdom and understanding exceeding much..."* (1 Kings 4:29, KJV).

God, the giver of all wisdom wants His children to study His word and apply the tenants to our daily lives. Given the aspirations of uniting with the right mate, we must allow the word of God to be our guiding roadmap. By committing to studying God's word and following His guidance, we will grow in the knowledge of our Lord.

The purpose of this *Workbook* is to provide you with the opportunity to apply the principles and concepts presented in *Women Stop the Chase: Let God's Man Find You*. You will have the chance to collaborate and expound on the topics and key points. Various exercises and discussion questions are used to enhance the readings in the main text.

This *Workbook* will also provide an excellent resource for women to use in individual or group bible study. The exercises can be adapted to complement the lesson or curriculum. The *Workbook* is specifically designed to mirror the chapters in the main text.

By using this *Workbook*, you will also be able to identify areas of personal and spiritual growth. The exercises will challenge you to examine your perspective and beliefs. Building your faith and trust in the King of Kings and Lord of Lords is the ultimate "take-away" from this *Workbook*.

The following exercises are designed to get you in the right frame of mind as we begin this journey of understanding God's pattern for relationships. As summarized earlier, the *Workbook* was developed to complement the text and not repeat the narrative. Therefore, it should be used primarily as a study aid with the main text.

If you are ready, then let's begin our journey together. I am excited about what our loving Heavenly Father is going to do along the way. How about you? Let's go!

Exercise 1

1. List five things that you would like to get out of reading the book and completing the *Workbook*?

    1) _____

    2) _____

    3) _____

    4) _____

    5) _____

2. Do you believe that God has a divine plan for establishing male and female relationships?

_____

_____

_____

_____

3. Proverbs 3:13-14 reminds us *that "Blessed are those who find wisdom, those who gain understanding, for she is more profitable than silver and yields better returns than gold"* (TNIV). Do you believe that God's wisdom is the foundation on which to build relationships?

_____

_____

_____

_____

_____

4. As a Christian woman, with respect to dating, has behavioral changes in society (i.e. social media) impacted "your" perspective on relationships?

_____
_____
_____
_____
_____
_____
_____
_____
_____
_____

Chapter 2: The Relationship Journey

In the book, *Women Stop the Chase: Let God's Man Find You*, there were several examples of how God brings relationships together. In addition, there were four main lessons which are summarized below:

1. God knows who and what we need in our lives.
2. Do not under estimate God's timing for doing things. He knows what is best.
3. Let the man [of God] initiate the pursuit. In essence, let him *find* you.
4. Let God create the heart connection between you and your potential mate. Don't try to create something that was never meant to be.

The following exercises are based primarily on the lessons learned. However, given the magnitude of the information presented in the main book, you may want to discuss these topics over the course of several study sessions.

Exercise 2

1. Based on the readings in this chapter, how would you describe God's pattern for relationships?

   _____

   _____

   _____

   _____

2. Do you believe that God knows who and what you need in your life?

   _____

   _____

   _____

3. Do you believe that God's timing is truly the best timing?

___

4. Are you willing to let God's man pursue you?

___

5. Are you willing to let God create the *heart connection* between you and the one He has for you?

_____

_____

_____

_____

_____

_____

_____

_____

_____

_____

_____

Chapter 3: Trusting God with the Decision

Proverbs 3:5-6 states, *"Trust in the Lord with all thine heart and lean not unto thine own understanding. In all thy ways acknowledge Him and He shall direct thy paths" (KJV).*

The focus of this chapter in the primary text was trusting God with our life decisions. There is an adage that says, "Ways and actions speak louder than words." I wonder what our ways and actions are saying about each of us when it comes to trusting God.

The following exercises are designed to challenge you to engage in critical thinking individually and with your study group. In addition, the questions will encourage you to spend quality and substantive time reflecting on your trust level in God.

Exercise 3

1. How would you define trust?

   _____

   _____

   _____

2. What does it mean to place your trust, confidence, faith, and hope in someone?

   _____

   _____

   _____

3. Sometimes, we say that we are trusting in God, yet our actions fail to align with the trust. Would you agree or disagree with this statement?

   _____

   _____

a. Do you trust God with decisions in your life?

_____

_____

_____

_____

_____

b. List examples of how you are trusting in Him?

_____

_____

_____

_____

4. Some people may think that adhering to Godly principles regarding relationships is "old-fashioned" and illogical. It is important to know what you believe and why. Take time to reflect below on what you believe.

_____

_____

_____

_____

_____

5. During the research for the book, I conducted an anonymous survey across the United States with 100 participants. The purpose of the survey was to explore the perceptions of individuals concerning women initiating relationships with men. Survey participants were asked, "If a man is seriously

interested in dating a woman, should he be the one to initiate the contact?" From a Christian perspective, what do you think and why?

_____

_____

_____

_____

6. Survey participants were also asked, "Should a woman pursue a man in a relationship?" What do you think and why?

_____

_____

_____

_____

7. The final question that the respondents were asked was, "Would you encourage your daughter to pursue a man in a relationship?" What would you recommend to your daughter?

_____

_____

_____

_____

_____

_____

_____

_____

Chapter 4: Pressing into the Things of God

If you are going to get anything from God, you are going to have to press your way into what God has for you. Spending time in prayer and fasting is expected when you are placing a demand on the things of God. In other words, a press of any kind requires action. It is easy to stand at the edge of the sea, but it takes faith to launch out into the deep.

The purpose of this chapter was to encourage you to press your way into the things of God. Regardless of circumstances, situations, or problems, don't allow them to dissuade you from seeking what God has already promised in His word.

The following exercises will give you the opportunity to reflect on your perspective of pressing into the things of God. I would encourage you to expound on this topic further in your study group.

Exercise 4

1. From your perspective, what does it mean to press?

   _____

   _____

   _____

2. How determined are you to receive from God?

   _____

   _____

   _____

3. In Genesis 32:26, Jacob wrestled with the angel in the wilderness. Jacob said, *"I will not let thee go, except thou bless me"* (KJV). What are you believing God for today?

   _____

   _____

   _____

4. In Luke 8:43-48, we find the recording of the woman with the issue of blood. She was plagued for 12 long years. Then she heard that Jesus was coming to town. Despite what people may have said to dissuade her from reaching Jesus, she was not to be deterred. Just imagine her pushing through the emotional and physical baggage of 12 years to get to Jesus. What baggage is stopping you from getting what God has for you?

_____

_____

_____

_____

5. Are you willing to press into the Kingdom of God for your blessings? Will you commit to the journey?

_____

_____

_____

Chapter 5: God's Precious Jewel

This chapter reminds us that we are God's precious jewels. He loves us more than we could ever imagine. He wants what is best for us according to His plan. As representatives of the Most High, we have a responsibility to become our best.

Since we all have areas in our lives that we want to improve, we can use various strategies and techniques to work on spiritual and personal development. For example, we can engage in consistent prayer, corporate bible study, retreats, personal study, etc. We can even apply techniques used in the military and business today.

As a retired military officer and a certified Green Belt in Lean Six Sigma, I was trained to use a technique called the Strength, Weakness, Opportunity, and Threat (SWOT) analysis tool. The analysis was initially conducted to help organizations evaluate their programmatic investments.

Although, the SWOT analysis tool has primarily been used in business, industry, and government assessments, I wonder what would happen if we conducted a SWOT analysis on ourselves?

Exercise 5: Part I

1. What are your strengths and weaknesses when it comes to spiritual and personal development?

_____

_____

_____

_____

_____

_____

2. Can you identify opportunities for growth?

_____

_____

_____

_____

3. What are some things that are threatening you from becoming what God designed you to be?

Exercise 5 Part II

1. What is your personal vision statement?

_____

_____

_____

_____

_____

2. Identify goals, and objectives for your personal growth plan. Ensure that your goals have metrics that you can successfully measure on a consistent basis. Many people use the SMART technique when designing goals. The acronym has changed over the years, but primarily means the following:

- ❖ S = Specific
- ❖ M = Measurable
- ❖ A = Attainable or Achievable
- ❖ R = Relevant or Realistic
- ❖ T = Time-bound or Timely

Whether spiritual or personal, it is essential that you develop goals so that you can have something to strive toward. Take time to write the goals down so that they are visible. For example, a goal could be: *By December 31, 2013, I will consistently read the bible daily.* Although this is a simple goal, it meets the SMART criteria. Write down your goals and objectives below.

_____

_____

_____

_____

_____

_____

_____

_____

_____

Chapter 6: Stepping Ahead of God?

Despite knowing that God will answer our prayer in His timing, sometimes we still want to expedite the process and help God out. For some reason, we think we know best. We will listen to friends, family, and even adopt some of society's habits. For a season, we may believe that everything is working fine. However, as time progresses, we realize the consequences of stepping ahead of God.

The main point of this chapter was to reiterate the importance of not stepping ahead of God's plan for our lives. Sometimes we rely solely on the heart to make decisions. However, we must trust and depend on God. He is the source of all wisdom.

The following exercises are designed to give you the opportunity to reflect on the degree in which you are waiting on the Lord versus stepping ahead of Him.

Exercise 6

1. Have you ever stepped ahead of God while praying for His will to be done?

_____

_____

_____

_____

_____

2. What is the difference between God's perfect will and His permissive will?

_____

_____

_____

_____

_____

3. Sometimes as women we might meet a man that for all intents and purposes we think is "Mr. Right." If he is not the one—we will try to make him the one. Despite early warning indicators, we invoke the big *ignore sign*. Has this situation ever happened to you?

_____

_____

_____

_____

4. When we step ahead of God, we invite unnecessary drama into our lives. We find ourselves going through emotional relationships that will eventually destroy our self-esteem. Have you ever experienced an unhealthy relationship based on operating outside of the will of God? What lessons did you learn?

_____

_____

_____

_____

5. Why is it important to wait on God? Are you stepping ahead of Him, or are you waiting on Him?"

_____
_____
_____
_____
_____
_____
_____
_____
_____
_____
_____
_____

Chapter 7: Are You Making Yourself Discoverable?

The purpose of this chapter was to challenge you to think about how prepared you are to receive God's man into your life. Despite the fact that we declare that we are ready to receive from God, sometimes we are not as prepared as we profess.

As indicated in this chapter, there are a series of questions that you can answer that will enable you to evaluate your current state. God knows your heart and "you." There is nothing hidden from the Master.

By answering these questions, you should have a better understanding of where you are in the preparation and waiting season. Ask the Holy Spirit to guide you in answering these questions. Be open and honest with yourself.

In the end, God knows if you are ready. His delay may mean that there is still work that needs to occur in you and your potential mate. Don't give up just commit to becoming the woman that God destined you to become.

Exercise 7

1. How is your relationship with God? Are you building a foundation in Him?

   _____

   _____

   _____

   _____

2. Do you truly desire to have a mate?

   _____

   _____

   _____

   _____

3. Are you ready to meet God's mate for you?

   _____

   _____

   _____

4. What are you doing to prepare?

___

5. If you were the *man*, would you be satisfied with you? Are there some things you need to change?

___

6. Are you the woman of excellence that God's man would be proud to introduce as his help-mate?

___

7. Are you allowing the Holy Spirit to let you know if this man is truly the one?

_____

_____

_____

8. Would you be proud to have him as the head of your household?

_____

_____

_____

9. How much do you know about this man?

_____

_____

_____

10. Is he a Christian?

_____

_____

11. Is he in a position to have a help-mate or family?

_____

_____

_____

12. Does he have a job or means to provide for a family?

_____

_____

_____

13. Does he even want to be married?

_____

_____

14. Do you have common goals and interests?

_____

_____

_____

15. Is the guy pursuing you or are you pursuing him?

_____

_____

_____

_____

_____

_____

16. Are the two of you compatible?

_____

_____

_____

_____

_____

_____

Appendix A

This appendix provides space for you to spend time in silent reflection. After having read this book, I want you to take time to write down the life lessons that will enable you to grow in God.

Appendix B

This appendix provides an opportunity for you to identify spiritual and personal goals that you would like to accomplish over the next year.

Appendix C

This appendix provides an opportunity for you to identify your **strengths**. What are your God-given gifts? Can you maximize those strengths in your life?

Appendix D

This appendix provides an opportunity for you to identify **weaknesses** that you would like to improve. It is not until we identify those areas, that we can actually begin to improve those areas.

Appendix E

This appendix provides an area for you to identify **opportunities** that will enable you to grow both spiritually and professionally.

Appendix F

This appendix provides an opportunity for you to identify those things that could **threaten** or prevent you from becoming the best that God designed you to be. For example, one can choose to settle for "not being good enough, when God has already designed you for greatness." Are your thoughts threatening your progress?

About the Author

Dr. Mary M. Gillam is a business owner, poet, motivational speaker, and retired Air Force Colonel with over 28 years of military service. After retiring from the military, Dr. Gillam worked as a government contractor for Booz Allen Hamilton. She was later appointed to the Senior Executive Service (SES) at the Office of the Secretary of Defense in the Pentagon where she served as the Director of Technology, Innovation and Engineering. After experiencing the entrepreneur bug, she decided to start her own company.

Dr. Gillam is currently the president and owner of M²G Dynamic Leadership Solutions, and the Mary M. Gillam Literary Enterprise, LLC. Both companies are service disabled veteran owned businesses.

A native of Roseboro, North Carolina, Dr. Gillam was raised by her paternal grandmother under very humble conditions. Her first book, *"I Never Said Good-bye"* was a special tribute to her grandmother who passed while she was stationed in Korea. The book is also a testament of Dr. Gillam's strong faith. Dr. Gillam is also the author of, *"A Jewel Collage of Poetry."*

Having spent over 30 years working in information systems, Dr. Gillam is the author of, *"Information Warfare: Combating the Threat in the 21st Century,"* and *"Exploring the Impact of the Clinger-Cohen Act of 1996 on Information Technology Governance."* A seasoned executive and servant-leader, Dr. Gillam is currently working on another book entitled, *"The CORE Leadership Development Model: 4 Steps to Releasing Your Leadership Potential."*

Dr. Gillam has a Bachelor of Science degree in Chemistry from North Carolina A&T State University, three Masters Degrees to include a Masters in Computers and Information Resource Management from Webster University. She also has a Graduate Certificate in Legislative Studies from Georgetown University, a Graduate Certificate in Project Management from Villanova, and a Doctorate in Management Information Systems Technology from the University of Phoenix. Dr. Gillam is a graduate of the military's Naval War College in Newport, RI, and the Air Command & Staff College in Montgomery, AL. She has been awarded multiple military and leadership awards to include the Spirit of the American Woman Leadership Award and the Federal Women's Executive Leadership Award. She also has a Green Belt in Lean Six Sigma.

Most importantly, Dr. Gillam is a born-again Christian. Having been called to Evangelism in September 1990, Dr. Gillam is currently enrolled in the Religious Education doctoral program at International Seminary in Florida.